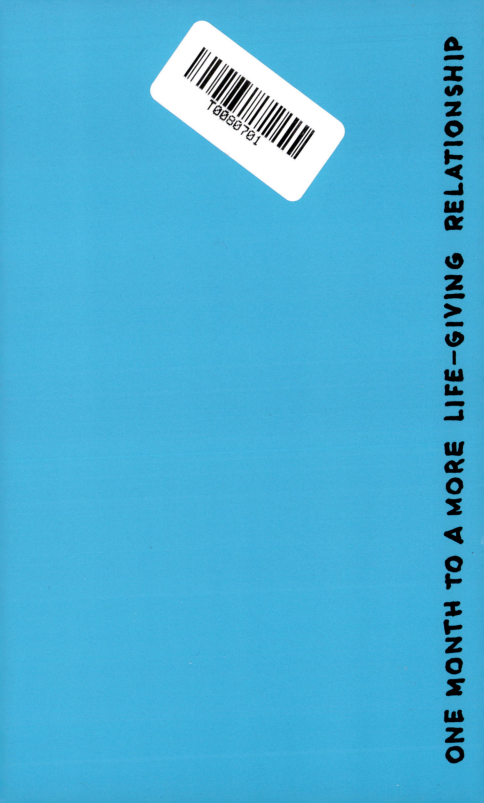

ONE MONTH TO A MORE LIFE-GIVING RELATIONSHIP

31

WAYS TO
SHOW HER
WHAT
LOVE IS

31
WAYS TO SHOW HER WHAT LOVE IS

One Month to a More
Life-giving Relationship

Jefferson Bethke

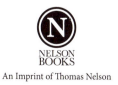

NELSON
BOOKS

An Imprint of Thomas Nelson

31 Ways to Show Her What Love Is

© 2022 Jefferson Bethke and Alyssa Bethke

Originally published as *31 Ways to Love and Encourage Her.*

Published in Nashville, Tennessee, by Nelson Books, an imprint of Thomas Nelson. Nelson Books and Thomas Nelson are registered trademarks of HarperCollins Christian Publishing, Inc.

Published in association with Yates & Yates, www.yates2.com.

Thomas Nelson titles may be purchased in bulk for educational, business, fundraising, or sales promotional use. For information, please e-mail SpecialMarkets@ThomasNelson.com.

Any internet addresses, phone numbers, or company or product information printed in this book are offered as a resource and are not intended in any way to be or to imply an endorsement by Thomas Nelson, nor does Thomas Nelson vouch for the existence, content, or services of these sites, phone numbers, companies, or products beyond the life of this book.

Scripture quotations are taken from the esv® Bible (The Holy Bible, English Standard Version®), copyright © 2001 by Crossway, a publishing ministry of Good News Publishers. Used by permission. All rights reserved.

ISBN 978-1-4002-2874-4 (eBook)
ISBN 978-1-4002-2868-3 (TP)

Library of Congress Control Number: 2021944963

Printed in the United States of America
22 23 24 25 26 LSC 10 9 8 7 6 5 4 3 2 1

CONTENTS

NOTE TO READERS

F irst off, you rock. By buying this book and going through it with your significant other, you obviously are already dominating at life! Alyssa and I have prayed over this project and really believe it can be a fun way to cultivate a healthy relationship and bring back the joy and intimacy that sometimes get lost amid the everyday activities.

To get the most out of this book, we'd first say *lean in*. Lean into the ideas, the spontaneity, and the parts that stretch you the most. Don't be afraid to just go for it. Have fun and create memories. These books were a collaborative effort, and we are firm believers that with this book (written from Jeff's perspective), as well as with *31 Ways to Show Him What Love Is* (written from Alyssa's perspective), whatever you put into it you will get out of it. Isn't that true with all our relationships as a whole? Also know that this is just a template. Some things won't be a good fit for your relationship or aren't doable based on certain locations, resources, and other variables.

We have tried to make every day as applicable for everyone as possible. With that being said, feel free to morph it, change it, adapt it—do whatever you need to do to get the most out of it. The goal isn't to rigidly follow this book and "cross each day off your checklist," but rather it's to bring a fresh vibrancy and life back into your relationship.

Also, a quick additional note to the dating folks out there. Obviously we are married, so we are coming from that perspective. But we also wanted to write this as a useful tool for dating couples. You might have to change it up in a different way. When not living together, some of these are a little harder to manage. Since you're dating, you probably don't see each other every single day. So feel free to stretch this out over a few months or pick just a few to do each week.

We're rooting for you!

PRAYER SUPPORT

Prayer is where the action is.

—JOHN WESLEY

Some of the most encouraging times in our marriage happen when Alyssa tells me she's praying for me. Not just in general but when she tells me what her prayer is. That she's praying for my walk with Jesus: that I'd come to know Him in a deeper way that day. She prays for my purity: that I'd protect and guard my thoughts and mind. She prays that God would give me wisdom in how to parent. And on. And on.

It makes me feel not alone. It makes me feel like during the bad days or the hard days or the days when I feel shame or temptation, I have an advocate. Not only is Alyssa in my corner, but most of all Jesus is. He stands with me and for me.

LOVE IN ACTION

- Ask your wife or girlfriend how you could pray for her.
- Sometime during the next week write out a prayer for her on a card or piece of paper and give it to her.
- Or ask if you can pray for her out loud.

YOUR THOUGHTS

HUMBLE APOLOGIES AND QUICK FORGIVENESS

Forgiveness says you are given another
chance to make a new beginning.

—DESMOND TUTU

Love in the real world means saying
you're sorry ten times a day.

—KATHIE LEE GIFFORD

Just a few hours ago (from the time I was typing this), Alyssa and I got into one of those little disagreements. You know, the ones where by the time you get to the end of them, you can't even remember what you were arguing about in the first place.

Actually, this one definitely was my fault. I had made a dumb side comment that was meant to be funny but in retrospect was just snarky and hurtful. When I made the comment, we were in the grocery store and just about to part ways to divide and conquer our shopping list (the only right way to do it, especially with kids. *Can I get an amen?*). While I was picking up my items, I had a few minutes to think about it. You know what I realized? It was simply my fault. I'd been wrong and what I said was hurtful. It was in that moment I felt bad and realized I needed to apologize and ask for forgiveness.

A couple of minutes later, after we reconvened, I said I was sorry. I asked her to forgive me. Then it hit me— forgiveness truly is one of the sustaining powers of a relationship. Without it, every relationship would venture into realms of resentment, hurt, bitterness, and more. And that stuff can destroy a relationship.

I'd say hands down one reason I think Alyssa and I have a relatively healthy relationship is that we both hold apologies and forgiveness as nonnegotiables. We've purposed that we will be humble enough to apologize and graceful enough to accept and speak forgiveness.

LOVE IN ACTION!

- Think of one thing you might not have apologized for, something you said, did, or have held on to today, yesterday, or maybe even a long time ago.
- Talk about forgiveness with your wife or girlfriend and discuss how you can integrate it more solidly into your relationship.

YOUR THOUGHTS

WALK, CHAT, AND RELAX

One of Alyssa's favorite things is to go for a walk. She usually goes every day, whether to just get outside or to get a good workout. To her, if she doesn't go for a walk, she feels a little pent up or stuck being inside all day.

I personally am not a huge fan of walks. I am more so now, but for a long time I pretty much hated them. I didn't like doing any physical activity that wasn't also fun at the same time, such as basketball or swimming.

I've started to change a little and now go with Alyssa on many of her walks. You know what's funny? There's something about taking a walk that just renews your energy and spirit for the day. It's strange, but there are some things that make for better conversations than others, like sitting up high on a water tower or going for a walk.

There are things we've talked about during our walks that have helped reset our focus. Or bring new energy and life to our relationship. Or it's just the pause needed to get a sense about how we are doing as a couple.

LOVE IN ACTION

- Go for a walk. Could be around the neighborhood or you could drive somewhere for a serious hike.
- Just walk and chat, hang out and relax.

YOUR THOUGHTS

DAY 4

CHOOSE A MONTHLY SCRIPTURE

> Think about it: when we read
> the Word, we place ourselves in
> the very presence of God.
>
> —ERIC METAXAS

The Scriptures are so powerful! They are active, living, and God's very own Word. They can breathe life into a relationship.

For Alyssa and me, Scripture is everything. Both of us try to read for at least a few minutes each day (even though with three young kids that is a challenge). Scripture anchors our relationship and reminds us of what's important.

Ultimately the more closely I follow Jesus, the better I can serve my wife. And the farther I drift from Jesus, the more I realize I'm not loving and serving my wife well.

A marriage or relationship that prioritizes the Scriptures as a center point is one that will flourish.

LOVE IN ACTION

— Select a Scripture passage to dwell on for the next month in regard to your relationship. It could be a verse to remind you to serve her better or it could be one you both choose as your "relationship verse" for the next month. For example, Ecclesiastes 4:9–12, John 13:34–35, or 1 Peter 4:8.

— Commit to discussing the chosen Scripture at least weekly, if not daily.

YOUR THOUGHTS

_____

_____

_____

_____

_____

_____

_____

_____

_____

_____

_____

_____

_____

_____

_____

_____

_____

_____

_____

_____

_____

_____

ACTS OF SERVICE

Accustom yourself continually to
make many acts of love, for they
enkindle and melt the soul.

—MOTHER TERESA

One of the best pieces of advice about marriage Alyssa and I received was to always remember that it's about giving, not taking. Or another way to put it: marriage is about serving, not about being served. But we structure our days and say and do certain things in hopes that we will be served or that we will get what we want.

If our girlfriend or wife doesn't do those things, we secretly start to get resentful or contemptuous. We start having that inner dialogue: *She should. . . . if only she. . . . I can't believe she expects me to always . . .*

One of the biggest joys in life can be to serve your wife or girlfriend. Service is secretly the key to joy. The reason I say "secret" is because most people haven't discovered it yet. Yes, it takes a little bit of time and energy. And sure, sometimes it feels harder than being served. Not many people, after doing something for someone, think, *Wow! Well, that was a total waste.* No. We realize it did something inside us. It created joy, not only in us, but in the person we served.

LOVE IN ACTION

- Do one act of service today for your girlfriend or wife.
- For me, this usually means I make the bed, give her a back rub, or give the kiddos a bath.
- Whatever you choose to do, serve her and then tell her how much joy it brings you.

YOUR THOUGHTS

LET LOOSE
AND DANCE

Alyssa and I are big fans of always playing music in the house. We usually turn on worship music in the morning and keep it playing in the background throughout the day. But when it's approaching dinner time, especially if I decide to hop in the kitchen and cook, we listen to something with a little more funk.

This usually means Taylor Swift, Justin Timberlake, Bruno Mars, and maybe some Justin Beiber. (Don't judge . . . because I know you're thinking about judging me right now. Is it too late now to say sorry?) And when a good song comes on, there's a good chance I'll grab Alyssa and start twirling her, dancing with her, and giving her a little old-school dip for the grand finale. My favorite part is that our daughter Kinsley absolutely loves it and giggles the whole time. There's something about dancing that brings with it joy and life.

LOVE IN ACTION

- Dance with her. It could be a funky, spontaneous dinner dance.
- Or when you're in the car, you could turn on some music and then get out and dance in the parking lot, driveway, or on the roadside for a few minutes. You could even go old school with some Macarena.
- Most of all, have fun with it! Don't be afraid to let loose and dance away.

YOUR THOUGHTS

IMPROVED COMMUNICATION SKILLS

Electric communication will never be
a substitute for the face of someone
who with their soul encourages
another person to be brave and true.

—CHARLES DICKENS

Words are but pictures of our thoughts.

—JOHN DRYDEN

Yesterday Alyssa and I had a little fight. *Disagreement* is probably a better word, but you know what I mean. It's what happens when the two of you are a little frustrated and you start getting that thought in your head, *I know*

I'm right. Why doesn't she_____? (You can fill in the blank.)

After the disagreement with Alyssa, I started to think about what had caused it and realized the topic wasn't the issue. We had disagreed because we hadn't properly communicated beforehand. And when we don't communicate, expectations are not understood or met, and that's usually ground zero for tension, strife, and more.

Often the disagreements aren't the actual problem. They are just the symptom. They are teaching us that something else is the real culprit—the real reason why there is frustration.

LOVE IN ACTION

- Ask her how you can communicate better.
- Ask if there are things you say or do that frustrate her.
- Revisit your past few disagreements and ask how you could have communicated better before they happened.

YOUR THOUGHTS

 *DAY 8*

RANDOM LOVE NOTES

Spread love everywhere you go.

—MOTHER TERESA

Sticky notes are the best things ever. They are good for to-do lists, daily reminders, or pranking your wife by putting them all over her car—or is that just me? (See Day 20.)

Words are powerful things. They can build up or they can tear down. Something about each new day brings the need for a new set of encouraging words. Alyssa and I share encouraging words in a million different ways. It might be my telling her things I enjoy about her or it might be her leaving sticky notes around the house naming things she appreciates about me.

LOVE IN ACTION

- Think of the top ten traits or qualities you love about your wife or girlfriend.
- Write each one down on a separate piece of paper.
- Randomly place the notes where she would normally see them during the day. For example, the nightstand, the bathroom mirror, the pantry, or on the speedometer in her car.

YOUR THOUGHTS

PRAYERFUL CHANGES

Consider how tough it is to change
yourself and you'll understand
what little chance you have in
trying to change others.

—JACOB M. BRAUDE

If that quote above isn't a smack to the face, I don't know what is. In a relationship, once the butterflies and puppy love start wearing off, you begin to notice things. Things that may annoy you, bother you, frustrate you, and upset you about the other person (and they certainly start to notice those things about you). One of the temptations is to want to change the person. You think *if only they would change this one thing, life would be a lot easier or better.* And while that might be the case, you should realize your efforts are probably futile.

Trying to change the other person for your benefit only brings more hurt, pain, and heartache. Now don't get me wrong, change is good and both of you will change over time, but Alyssa and I have noticed changes are best that come through prayer and the Holy Spirit. Instead of telling Alyssa about something I think needs to change, I start praying and ask God to either: (a) show Alyssa the area she needs to change or (b) show me where maybe there is an area I need to grow in. It might be harder, but it's better than trying to change Alyssa.

LOVE IN ACTION

- Think of one thing you would like to change about your wife or girlfriend.
- Really dig deep and ask in what ways *you* could change on that issue? (For example, I hate making the bed and Alyssa loves to make the bed. We fought about it off and on for the first year of our marriage. I tried so hard to change her. And finally God convicted me and said if she wanted it made, then I should serve and love her in that way. So now the bed gets made every morning, and I haven't brought it up since.

YOUR THOUGHTS

DAY 10

CREATE A
RELATIONSHIP
JOURNAL

One of my favorite things Alyssa and I do each week is get away for about an hour and go through what we call our "marriage journal." Alyssa's parents watch the kiddos and we head off to the beach or somewhere restful and go through the journal. We keep a journal that has five to seven questions we ask ourselves each week and then we record the answers in the journal. It's changed the dynamic of our relationship in regard to communicating well, squashing certain things before they turn big, and simply understanding more about each other. Also, it's fun to have a written record of our relationship and how we did in different seasons.

A friend gave us this idea along with suggested questions, and we have loved doing it ever since. The cool part is you have full control over whether to change it up or keep the same format and questions we use.

The questions we ask are:

- What brought you joy this week?
- What's something that was hard this week?
- Is there anything that's gone unsaid this week?
- What dream or thought has been on the forefront of your mind this week?
- What's one specific thing I can do for you in the week ahead?
- How can I pray for you in the week ahead?

And then once a month we ask ourselves how our finances and sex life are doing.

In all honesty, doing this journal has been life changing for us. I get to hear how Alyssa's week has been hard when maybe I hadn't been paying attention all that well. Also I get to hear how I can serve her in the week ahead.

LOVE IN ACTION

- Today find a journal around the house or pick up a brand-new one.
- Game plan how you and your wife or girlfriend are going to manage your relationship journal and either keep or edit the questions we provided.
- Commit to getting away and spending one hour together on your journal each week.

YOUR THOUGHTS

_____

_____

_____

_____

_____

_____

_____

_____

_____

_____

_____

_____

_____

_____

_____

_____

_____

_____

_____

_____

_____

_____

_____

BUILD A
FUN FORT

I was in love with making forts as a kid. I'd get all the sheets, pillows, chairs, and anything else I could use from around the house to build intricate forts right in the middle of the living room. My mom wasn't always a huge fan (for the simple fact the whole house looked like a tornado went through it), but she let me do it nonetheless.

There's something about making a fort that creates a fun sense of adventure and imagination. In fact, that's one thing I think we are sorely lacking these days, especially in romantic relationships. Imagination is no longer a thing celebrated. Creativity is no longer a muscle we routinely work out. Imagination and creativity are seen as traits to be left in childhood.

What if I told you creativity, adventure, and imagination are sometimes the keys to a fun and healthy relationship? Thinking outside of the box, mixing it up every once in a while, and doing things you wouldn't normally do can help jumpstart a relationship.

LOVE IN ACTION

- Today build a fort with her. Make it as elaborate or simple as you want. That's the fun part. You get to be a kid again and there's no grade after you're done building.
- Work together and laugh along the way.
- And when it's done, hang out inside your fort and tell stories.

YOUR THOUGHTS

Day 12

REVISIT DATING ETIQUETTE

Manners are a sensitive awareness of the feelings of others.

—EMILY POST

When you first start dating, you're on your best behavior. You do and say things to impress her but also shower kindness on her. For example, it's common gentlemanly etiquette to open the door for her, pull out her chair, bring flowers, and more.

For some reason if you've been dating or married for any length of time, this stuff starts to wane. The etiquette fades or no longer happens. But shouldn't it be the opposite? If the love and connection is growing, shouldn't that stuff at least stay the same or grow as well?

I know for me, I get really comfortable with Alyssa, thinking, *Oh, she already knows how much I love her.* I become complacent. She does know that I love her, but active pursuit is different from complacency. One leads to a flourishing relationship, and the other doesn't.

LOVE IN ACTION

- Ask yourself what you can bring back that you did when you were first dating.
- What small gesture can you continually make as an encouragement to her? Maybe that means opening the door for her again, bringing her flowers, or complimenting her.

YOUR THOUGHTS

ENCOURAGE
HER DREAMS

Hold fast to dreams, for if dreams die,
life is a broken-winged bird that cannot fly.

—LANGSTON HUGHES

Alyssa and I were only dating at the time but I remember when she mentioned she was looking for a new hobby. Photography was one of those possible hobbies, so I filed it away and waited to see if any of those listed possibilities bubbled back up. And again, photography did. She really wanted to start getting into it but didn't have a camera. I was broke and couldn't buy her one, but she had a good steady job and, soon enough, bought a camera. A few months went by and she started to get really involved with her new hobby, but her camera needed a better lens.

I started saving and researching options. I had some photography friends I texted and messaged about the best lenses. Finally I bought a lens and surprised her with it. What's awesome is she's been able to take pictures of friends, families, and others with that camera, using that lens.

In a relationship each person will have dreams, hopes, and future plans. It could be a skill to develop or something to gather funds for.

Maybe your wife or girlfriend wants to learn more cooking skills. Maybe she wants to learn to play the guitar. Think back on recurring themes over the past few weeks or months of your relationship. What is something she wants to accomplish but hasn't pursued yet? Whatever that is, do something toward it.

LOVE IN ACTION

— Encouragement could mean buying her a special cookbook or finding free YouTube videos on cooking for her to watch.
— Write out a card or note about how much you love to see her chase her passions and dreams and how you're her biggest cheerleader.

YOUR THOUGHTS

_____

_____

_____

_____

_____

_____

_____

_____

_____

_____

_____

_____

_____

_____

_____

_____

_____

_____

_____

_____

_____

_____

_____

 *DAY 14*

THOUGHTFUL SURPRISES

When Alyssa was in the hospital giving birth to Kannon, our second child, I was with them, but as the dad, I did a good amount of sitting around while Alyssa did all the work. And I don't know about you, but when I sit around I basically just want to eat.

Food.

Lots of it.

Alyssa could sense this and told me to open her overnight bag. When I looked inside, I saw one of my favorite snacks—peanut butter M&M's, for those wondering. I immediately felt so loved. Why? Because she had thought of me beforehand. It probably cost Alyssa eighty cents and about fifteen seconds of extra time when she went to the grocery store the week before. But to me, it was this tiny but amazing moment of feeling special and understood, like she knew me.

(Well, I also get hungry a lot, so I guess it was in her best interest to keep me fed.)

LOVE IN ACTION

- Think of your wife's or girlfriend's favorite treat. Or coffee drink. Then surprise her with it.
- When she asks why, say, "No reason, I was just thinking of you."

YOUR THOUGHTS

INTENTIONAL COMPLIMENTS

I can live for two months on
a good compliment.

—MARK TWAIN

We've mentioned before that words are potent things with immense power. I've noticed lately, though, that compliments have different levels of power based on who they come from. A stranger might compliment me and I'm encouraged, but when Alyssa compliments me it does so much more. Why? Because I'm close to Alyssa and she's the love of my life. When the person who loves you and knows you still compliments you, that has power.

Robert Brault once said, "There is no effect more disproportionate to its cause than the happiness bestowed by a small compliment." Isn't that so true? It's an easy thing, yet it can bring such an enormous amount of blessing.

Words give life. They encourage and build up.

LOVE IN ACTION

- Be intentional about complimenting your wife or girlfriend today.
- Every time you offer her a compliment, write out the compliment on your phone or on a piece of paper.
- At the end of the day, give her the note listing all the compliments to show her how much you care about her and to reinforce the life you spoke over her today.

YOUR THOUGHTS

 *DAY 16*

WRITE HER
A LETTER

Letters are among the most
significant memorial a person
can leave behind them.

—JOHANN WOLFGANG VON GOETHE

There's something about a handwritten note that seems especially thoughtful and memorable. You could say the same thing in a letter that you say in a text, and the letter would feel more tangible and worth saving.

In fact, Alyssa to this day still has all the letters I wrote her over the years. I even used to spray my cologne on some of the letters when we were dating long distance so that when she opened the envelope it would smell a little like me. I know, I know, my game was on point at that stage in my life. Thank goodness we didn't start dating in middle school or else those letters would smell like Axe body spray (middle school boys' locker room forever).

Letters have a way of making you, the writer, think things through or say things a little differently. A letter received in the mail is definitely the most exciting. This is hard, though, when you are married because you live in the same house. This is why today's challenge is a fun one. Basically, you are creating a time capsule.

LOVE IN ACTION

- Write her a letter. Then get two envelopes and two stamps.
- Mail the letter to a friend or a parent who can hold on to it for a little bit.
- After a few weeks or months have that person put the letter in the other envelope addressed to her and mail it. What a fun surprise when she opens the mailbox and discovers your thoughtfulness.

YOUR THOUGHTS

DISCUSS AND EMBRACE THE HARD TIMES

There are no bonds so strong as those which are formed by suffering together.

—HARRIET ANN JACOBS

If someone were to ask me what Alyssa and I have gone through in our marriage that helped us grow the most or strengthened us, the answer would no doubt be the hard things. Relationships, financial issues, tough news we got from a friend, and so forth.

It's hard walking through difficult times, but, looking back, there is something special about hardships that acts as a glue when walked through together.

49

Of course that doesn't mean we should go hunting for hardships. It also doesn't mean we should avoid them. So many times in relationships we try to do everything in our power to take the easiest road, make the easiest decision, or do whatever will cause the least amount of tension or require the least degree of toughness.

What if instead of dreading those hard moments, we embraced them? What if we didn't search them out but when they landed on our doorstep, we welcomed them as moments to grow together in a way that prosperity or success never could grow us?

LOVE IN ACTION

— Reflect on a hardship you and your wife or girlfriend have gone through together.
— Talk about how you grew closer and what you learned from the hardship.

YOUR THOUGHTS

Day 18

MAKE FOOD
CONNECTIONS

Eating is so intimate. It's very sensual.
When you invite someone to sit at your
table and you want to cook for them,
you're inviting a person into your life.

—MAYA ANGELOU

love food. Like, seriously, *love food*. For example, I have
a minor obsession with Chipotle . . . that guac though!
Alyssa and I believe in eating good food—having good
meals—while enjoying good conversation. Food is something that really ties together our relationship.

Food is almost always at the center of our adventures.
(Just take a peek at our scrapbooks!) We remember most

adventures and trips by where we ate and what restaurant was the best.

Most of us eat around three meals a day: breakfast, lunch, and dinner. Sadly, in our culture we've made food more about worship or efficiency. We either worship the food (place way more importance on it than it deserves) or we see it as nutrients only (we count calories, we do the math, etc.). Neither viewpoint is correct. Food is an incredible, beautiful gift from our Creator and is a natural relationship builder. That's why most of us feel slightly weird eating alone. I'll be honest though. I'm pretty introverted, and I like a solo meal, just like I enjoy going to the movies alone, but I digress.

Food is an opportunity to sit at the table, look your table companions in the eye, and build relationships. You love, laugh, cry, and grow closer at the table. And preparing the food can be lots of fun!

LOVE IN ACTION

- Use food today in a way that builds your relationship. That could mean cooking a meal for her.
- Or it could mean taking your wife or girlfriend out to her favorite restaurant.
- It could also mean together trying something unique, food you have never tasted before, just to have fun. Whatever it is, use food for what it is today—an easy opportunity to grow closer to the person across the table.

YOUR THOUGHTS

CARE FOR HER CAR

You can tell a lot by a looking inside a person's car. If you looked inside mine, you'd realize I have three kids (three car seats), I'm not *that* clean—not as organized as with my house, and I like a good air freshener. For a lot of people their car is a second home, since they use it every day to get to work, run errands, and more.

I still remember mine and Alyssa's cars when we were dating. Oh, how many memories those cars hold. Our first dates, many late-night drives to get food, and, of course, our epic listening sessions—old Disney songs or NSYNC throwbacks—and when I blew out a speaker in mine.

LOVE IN ACTION

- Today the challenge is to do something with the car that serves her.
- That could mean washing her car. It could mean vacuuming the inside of the car.
- Or it could mean simply leaving little notes all around the car (the dashboard, the glovebox, under the seat, in the trunk).

YOUR THOUGHTS

START A FRIENDLY PRANK WAR

Lighthearted pranks can make an amazing memory. It might just be my personality, but I've always been a huge fan. For example, one of my favorites was when I put my friend's car on Craigslist with a super cheap price and he got a phone call every two to three minutes for a week straight. Or little things like trying to scare Alyssa when she comes around a corner.

Pranks, if done right, have a way of creating a fun little memory. If she has an iPhone, you can screen-capture her home screen, make that picture the new background picture, and put all the apps on the second page so now it looks like she has a frozen home screen. You could also put a toy spider or snake somewhere in the cupboard (actually, if she is anything like Alyssa she will *hate* this one, so use discretion). Basically do something that is harmless, fun, and does no damage.

LOVE IN ACTION

- Do something you think will make her laugh. And who knows? You just might start a friendly couple's prank war!

YOUR THOUGHTS

SURPRISE
SWITCH-UPS

A lyssa and I have a pretty good rhythm in our home. You know, who normally takes out the trash, who does the grocery shopping, and other things. For example, I'm the kitchen-cleaner-upper. Why? Because I'm a little OCD about organization. (I'm that guy who likes vacuuming the carpet because of the lines it makes after you're done.) So that means I do the dishes, wipe down the counters, put the leftover food away, and so on.

And Alyssa is in charge of grocery shopping and meal planning. Now, of course, neither of these is so rigid we can't jump in and help out each other every once in a while. But we usually do the things we've learned mesh well with our relationship.

LOVE IN ACTION

- Today, think about one thing that is her "normal" responsibility that you can take on to surprise her. This could be making the bed, doing the shopping, taking the trash out, or feeding the dog.
- For the dating couples reading this, you will probably have to get a little more creative since you aren't in the same home to be able to have a ton of different opportunities. But maybe if she usually chooses the restaurant (or some other activity), you could surprise her by designing a special date.

YOUR THOUGHTS

CREATE A
THANKFUL LIST

It's not happy people who are thankful,
it's thankful people who are happy.

—ANONYMOUS

couldn't agree more with the opening quote. Most people don't realize that thankfulness is actually the secret to joy. The reason I call it a secret is it seems many haven't caught on yet! In the Bible thankfulness is elevated almost to the place of being the heart of worship.

A thankful heart is exactly what God is looking for and is pleased with. When we are thankful it brings Him glory and us joy. In fact, the Bible even says that thankfulness is the will of God! (1 Thessalonians 5:18).

A lot of times we think the will of God is this mystical

thing—like what passion or career we should pursue—when the Bible says just being thankful is His will. I've seen this to be true in my relationship with Alyssa. I'm serving her the best, loving her the best, and being fulfilled the most in our relationship when I'm thankful and on the hunt for things to be thankful for.

LOVE IN ACTION

- Hunt for things you are thankful for about her and write each one down. Feel free to even mark the littlest things. By the end of the day, you should have dozens of things you are thankful for, if not hundreds!
- Dwell on the list during the evening and maybe even show her or read to her the list of all the reasons you are thankful for her.

 *DAY 23*

ENCOURAGEMENT VIA INTERNET POSTS

Correction does much, but
encouragement does more.

—JOHANN WOLFGANG VON GOETHE

A word of encouragement from
a spouse can save a marriage.

—JOHN C. MAXWELL

One of the cool things about the internet is it gives you a perspective on things being bigger than just you. I've found, seen, or been a part of some of the coolest little communities online. They have encouraged one another, helped one another financially, and built things for underprivileged folks around the world. Sometimes the internet gets a bad rap, but I think it's at its strongest when a community is coming together in a way they couldn't have offline because they are scattered all around the world.

Now I'm not a huge fan of the person who pretty much does social media PDA (you know what I'm talking about, unless maybe that's you). You know, that old friend who posts pictures of his wife or girlfriend making out with him in every other picture. It's like, bro, take that offline. But there is a space for treating your platform online as a natural extension of your life offline. And if there is someone you love and care about in real life, it makes sense that person would show up online sometimes.

LOVE IN ACTION

— Share three things about your wife or girlfriend you are thankful for, or recount your story in a picture caption.
— Post a picture of your wife or girlfriend along with some encouraging words.
— Use the hashtag #31creativeways so folks can see the power of a community that believes in relationships and lifting up one another!

YOUR THOUGHTS

SEND CHEESY PICKUP LINES

'm a big fan of cheesiness. I'm the king of bad jokes, and I love the most ridiculous pickup lines. Just ask Alyssa. At this point she barely laughs, and she makes a face that communicates, "Man, I sure got lucky marrying this guy."

My favorite thing to do is surprise her with pickup lines or bad jokes all throughout the day, especially when she least expects it. We haven't even gotten out of bed and I'll say, "Do you have a Band-Aid? Because I scraped my knee falling for you."

There's something about these silly lines that brings joy and spontaneity to our relationship and is a lot of fun. It makes her laugh, and you know there's nothing better than when you can make your wife or girlfriend laugh.

LOVE IN ACTION

- Hop on Google and find ten of your favorite cheesy pick-up lines.
- Use them throughout the day.
- Say them, write them down, or text them to her. Watch out! She will probably fall in love with you all over again!

YOUR THOUGHTS

REVIEW YOUR RELATIONSHIP STORY

> Who cares about the clouds when
> we're together? Just sing a song
> and bring the sunny weather.
>
> —DALE EVANS

> A person isn't who they are during
> the last conversation you had with
> them—they're who they've been
> throughout your whole relationship.
>
> —RAINER MARIA RILKE

Stories are powerful. Whether we realize it or not, we think in story. We are not mindless computers absorbing data. We give that data flesh. The data gets humanized. It gets storied. And a lot of times, story is the very way we remember our past and look toward the future. As a couple, we know this is true. We don't see our relationship as random, abstract things but instead as the crazy story of how two lives intersected and never were the same again.

I mean, if you've been together for any length of time, you will often be asked about your story, and it becomes easy to memorize your response. The cookie-cutter version. I realized the other day that every time I tell Alyssa's and my story, I feel a little spark of joy and gratitude that I ended up with her.

There's something about recounting your story that strengthens your relationship. The good, the bad, the easy, the hard, the breakup, the kids, the first date, or that awkward first kiss. (Which Alyssa and I definitely had. That's a story for another time though.)

LOVE IN ACTION

- Whether it's when you put down the kids at night or on a coffee date in the morning, go back over your story soon.
- There's always more to learn, so try to ask questions about details you've wondered about.
- Talk about the hard times so far. Talk about the good times so far.
- Then the most fun part, I think, is talking about when you will have this discussion again in, say, ten years. What do you want your story to be then? What do you want the next ten years to look like?

YOUR THOUGHTS

MAKE HER LAUGH

Laughter is carbonated holiness.

—ANNE LAMOTT

It's true. There's something about laughter that is downright sacred. When you're laughing, there's joy you can't explain. It does something to you. It warms your heart. Another favorite quote of mine is from George Gordon Byron, "Always laugh when you can. It's cheap medicine."

It's an understatement to say Alyssa and I love to laugh. I'm always doing something dumb around the house. Making up a song of sorts or talking in weird accents that I create. (Frankly, if anyone other than Alyssa saw these antics, they'd probably think I was crazy.) Laughter is something that connects us. Brings us closer together. Cultivating joy can actually be a strengthening and bonding agent in a relationship.

Be creative!

LOVE IN ACTION

- How can you make your woman laugh today? Maybe it's as simple as reading the jokes on the back of a Laffy Taffy wrapper. (Let's be honest; those are the best anyway.)
- Or maybe you do some funny dance or playful antic right after dinner. Your goal today is to make her laugh!

YOUR THOUGHTS

ENTER HER WORLD

There are only two forces that
unite men—fear and interest.

—NAPOLEON BONAPARTE

I absolutely love *Back to the Future*. It's my favorite movie of all time. In my office I have a *Back to the Future* poster, Marty and Doc figurines, as well as a now-discontinued DeLorean Lego set. To say I'm a fan is an understatement. In fact, I always know other fans based on my constant use of one-liners from the film. ("There's that word again: *heavy*. Why are things so heavy in the future? Is there a problem with the earth's gravitational pull?") I know they *aren't* fans if I drop a line and they just stare blankly.

Shortly after we married, I asked whether my wife was a BTTF fan, too, but to my surprise, she hadn't seen the movie yet. We ended up watching it on our honeymoon and

I could tell she thought it was fun, but she didn't think it was life changing, like I did. If my memory serves me correctly, we've even watched it since then, but I won't tell you how many times. Alyssa isn't a huge fan, but she continues rewatching it.

Why? Because she wants to enter into my world. She wants to know the one-liners so she can use them to connect with me. She wants to watch the movie because she wants to get closer to me.

Entering into your wife's or girlfriend's world is vital to a healthy relationship. It always saddens me when I see a couple and it's very much a "he does his thing, she does her thing" type of relationship. Good relationships enter into each other's spaces.

How can you enter her world today?

LOVE IN ACTION

- Research something your wife or girlfriend is interested in and have a fun conversation about it while you eat a meal.
- Get a pedicure with her. Seriously! This one really isn't all that bad, even though guys sometimes hate on it. Someone cleaning my feet, making them look good, and then ending it all with a foot massage? Fine by me!

YOUR THOUGHTS

ASK AND *LISTEN*

> Listen with the intent to understand,
> not the intent to reply.
>
> —STEPHEN COVEY

By nature, I'm a fixer. I like to tinker with things, take them apart, put them back together. When something doesn't go the way I planned, I start analyzing it and wondering *how I can fix it*. This is a good trait most of the time (you know, when I'm building something or trying to solve a problem). But if I'm not careful, this can be hurtful to Alyssa.

Whenever she is feeling down, something bad happened, or she just needs to talk, the last thing she wants me to do is try to fix it. In fact, she'll even say in some of our discussions, "Don't try to fix it, just *listen*." Now, of course, I'm just trying to be helpful when I try to solve her problem, but I'm trying to be helpful on *my* terms, not hers.

81

To truly love someone, you must learn to love them on their terms. Meaning you offer encouragement, blessing, love, and kind words in a way that they best receive, not the way you best receive or *you* want to give.

For Alyssa—and for most but not all girls—listening is huge. They want to feel listened to. Heard. Seen. (Shoot, this isn't just a girl thing because I guess I'm that way too. It's natural to want to feel understood.)

So how can you listen better today?

LOVE IN ACTION

- Make a special point to talk more slowly.
- Ask double the number of questions you usually do. For example, ask, "Can you tell me more about that?" or "Why do you like that?" or "Why do you feel that way?"

FACEBOOK (AND OTHER) MESSAGES

I remember stalking Alyssa on Facebook before I met her. We had a mutual friend and Alyssa had caught my eye. I'd visit her Facebook page and scroll through pictures. It took a while, but I finally gathered the courage to send her a message. This was in 2009, and I can still go into my Facebook account and see that first message.

The fun part (or the bad part) about the internet is it leaves a lasting trail. It's like a time capsule. So use it to your advantage.

LOVE IN ACTION

— Message your girl with a sweet, romantic note.
— If you don't have Facebook, get creative. Write her an email, leave an Instagram comment, or something similar.
— If sending messages over the internet is not your thing, go old-school and send a card.

YOUR THOUGHTS

MUSIC PLAYLISTS

Music can change the world
because it can change people.

—BONO

Where words fail, music speaks.

—HANS CHRISTIAN ANDERSEN

Alyssa and I both came of age or were teenagers at the end of the '90s and beginning of the 2000s. Because of this, we were in the glory days for music playlists. Back then a playlist wasn't just something you made quickly on your iPhone, but it was incredibly carefully thought out and structured. You then burned it onto a CD for your significant other. (Please tell me I'm not the only one remembering this right now.)

Now, I don't want to be the person who is always like,

"Well, back in *my day*!" That is classic dad syndrome. But there was something special that has been lost about the making of music mixes we'd gift to each other. I still remember a few different ones I made for Alyssa while we were dating. There was even one I made during our breakup that I gave to her after we got back together.

LOVE IN ACTION

- Whether it's an iPhone playlist or a CD you burn, make your wife or girlfriend a playlist today. Be thoughtful with the theme. Either songs that remind you of her, that tell your story from the beginning, or songs that you hope represent your relationship.
- Plan a special time to present her with your gift.

YOUR THOUGHTS

FOOT-WASHING AFFECTION

I still remember the day I proposed to Alyssa. I asked two friends to go to a secluded beach where they'd set the scene before we arrived. They scattered rose petals, lit candles, and hung up pictures from our relationship, lining the pathway from the car down to the beach.

And when we got to the beach, there was a blanket spread out and a bottle of champagne. It's hard for me to remember every little detail because it was such a blur—I was so nervous. One thing I do remember is that before I proposed, I got down on my knees, took out a thermos of warm water and a washcloth from my backpack and began to wash her feet. I told her I wanted this to be a symbol of our relationship, of my serving her and lifting her up in every regard . . . and then I asked her to marry me.

There's something about foot washing that is incredibly humbling. It feels a little awkward, yet holy. For thousands of years it's been a picture of service, originating in antiquity when foot washing was a necessity in many desert climates.

While it might not be as needed functionally, it's still just as powerful a picture of care and affection.

LOVE IN ACTION

- Wash your wife's or girlfriend's feet today.
- Make it super special by writing a little letter you read to her or setting up a picnic for her afterward.
- Let her know how much you care and how much you enjoy serving her.

YOUR THOUGHTS

YOUR TURN

You didn't think there was going to be a Day 32 did ya? We thought we'd add one more day and turn it over to you. Think of something you could do for your significant other today.

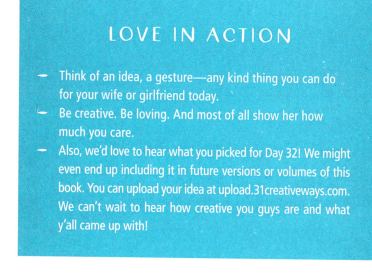

LOVE IN ACTION

— Think of an idea, a gesture—any kind thing you can do for your wife or girlfriend today.

— Be creative. Be loving. And most of all show her how much you care.

— Also, we'd love to hear what you picked for Day 32! We might even end up including it in future versions or volumes of this book. You can upload your idea at upload.31creativeways.com. We can't wait to hear how creative you guys are and what y'all came up with!

YOUR THOUGHTS

AFTERWORD

F irst off, you all rock! For reals. Complete rock stars. Why? Because you care about your relationship. You're investing in it. You believe in it. It matters to you.

We believe that a relationship is like a garden. For it to flourish it needs proper nourishment, constant care, and an awareness of the things trying to hurt it, and sometimes it gets a little messy. This book is just a start to hopefully continuing or taking that leap of putting you and your wife or girlfriend on the path to a vibrant and beautiful relationship.

So thank you for taking this journey with us. Thank you for reading this book. And thank you for just being you. We'd love to hear from you and how the challenge went by sharing something online with the hashtag #31creativeways. We are constantly on that hashtag to see all the awesome stuff you guys are doing and ways you tweaked one of our challenges to make it work for you.

We love when folks give us a shout on social media, so feel free to stop by and say hey!

Would love to e-meet you.

STOP BY AND SAY HI!

Instagram and Twitter:
@jeffersonbethke and @alyssajoybethke

Facebook:
fb.com/jeffersonbethkepage and fb.com/alyssajoybethke

Snapchat:
jeffersonbethke

Website:
jeffandalyssa.com

ABOUT THE
AUTHORS

Jefferson and Alyssa Bethke live in Maui with their three kids: Kinsley, Kannon, and Lucy. They write books (including *Jesus > Religion*, *It's Not What You Think*, *Love Is*, *To Hell with the Hustle*, *Take Back Your Family*, *Spoken For*, and *Satisfied*), make online videos, and host a podcast or two. Their mission is to equip and encourage people to follow Jesus in their day-to-day. They have a yellow lab named Aslan and enjoy reading good books and drinking good coffee during their downtime.

You can read more at JeffandAlyssa.com.

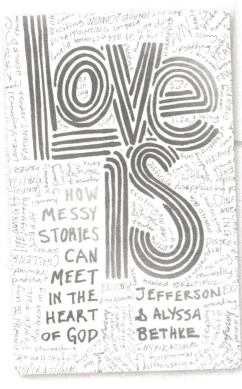